Mary's Quilt Garden

10 Floral Block Projects

JENNY RUNDLE

Schiffer Publishing Ltd®
4880 Lower Valley Road • Atglen, PA 19310

Other Schiffer Books on Related Subjects:

Making the Lancaster Diamond Sampler: A 19th Century Quilt Design by Fanny's Friend, 978-0-7643-4549-4, $39.99

Trip Around the World: A Country Quilt Block Travelogue, 978-0-7643-4000-0, $24.99

Library of Congress Control Number: 2013947542

Type set in Adobe Jenson Pro/Ajile

ISBN: 978-0-7643-4462-6
Printed in The United States of America

Published by Schiffer Publishing, Ltd.
4880 Lower Valley Road
Atglen, PA 19310
Phone: (610) 593-1777; Fax: (610) 593-2002
E-mail: Info@schifferbooks.com

For our complete selection of fine books on this and related subjects, please visit our website at **www.schifferbooks.com**. You may also write for a free catalog.

This book may be purchased from the publisher. Please try your bookstore first.

We are always looking for people to write books on new and related subjects. If you have an idea for a book, please contact us at **proposals@schifferbooks.com**.

Schiffer Publishing's titles are available at special discounts for bulk purchases for sales promotions or premiums. Special editions, including personalized covers, corporate imprints, and excerpts can be created in large quantities for special needs. For more information, contact the publisher.

I dedicate this book to my husband Doug.... Thank you for putting up with my hobby over the years and the many times I have gone away to visit shows both in the UK and overseas and left you on your own at home.

To my wonderful friend, Mary Short, a quilter of many years with whom I have shared many happy times and adventures.

CONTENTS

Mary's Garden

Mary, Mary, quite contrary
How does your garden grow?
With silver bells
And cockle shells
And pretty maids all in a row

~ *An old English nursery rhyme*

Hortus conclusus, the "enclosed garden" or Mary's Garden, was a place of beauty and pleasure, dating from medieval times. It was a sacred area that might represent the Christian soul, enclosed in the body, or the Church, and formed of the body of the faithful. The *hortus conclusus* was an allegorical representation of the Virgin Mary: its enclosed nature taken to mean virginity, whilst each flower planted in the garden represented one of her virtues. The white Madonna Lily represented the Annunciation, the violet her modesty; the red rose the Virgin Mary herself.

It was the monks who created the sophisticated designs that is still typical of many cottage gardens today. The paths were often constructed in the shape of a Cross to emphasize the meditative aspects of the monks' work. The Cross was supplemented by a beautiful rose bush in the center of a circular bed surrounded by a low evergreen hedge. After the Reformation, attempts were made to destroy the traditional link between plants and worship. Mary plants, such as Our Lady's thimble and herb of the Madonna, returned to their original names of harebell and costmary. As the mother of Christ, Mary was honored by having a number of plants named after her: Lavender — Breath of Paradise — had no scent until Mary, it was said, laid Jesus' swaddling clothes on the bush; White Lily — emblem of majesty and purity; Madonna Lily — Mary was visited by Gabriel with a spray of lilies in his hands. The lily is also a symbol of resurrection and is the Easter flower.

Plants have had symbolic as well as utilitarian meanings since the beginning of civilization. With the coming of Christianity, churches often developed on the sites of pre-Christian and Celtic holy places, which had customs of their own. The missionaries had two choices — as with other customs, they could suppress it or adopt it — and it seems they adopted the second course, so instead of a Pagan Spring festival a Christian festival was held in honor of the Virgin Mary. Plants played a focal point in these ceremonies, as the monks would decorate the church on feast days and festivals with the appropriate plants. Many species became naturalized from wreathes and posies that were left on graves or used as flower arrangements inside the church.

Many of the flowers in the book are based on Mary's Garden, but others could have been found in Medieval English gardens or the countryside. Some now are in danger of disappearing completely and join the growing list of extinct flora and fauna. The blocks made from this book may become part of history in time; not only in the history of the quilt and fabrics used, but also as a valuable source of flowers in our time.

Introduction

The designs in this book can be used to make a single flower for a cushion, a small wall-hanging using nine blocks, or, using a combination of the blocks, a larger wall-hanging. Making the borders with sashing will allow you to make a quilt any size you wish. You can choose your own blocks, setting, and size to make your own unique Mary's Garden quilt.

The patterns are not difficult to follow, but if you have knowledge of basic appliqué skills either by machine or hand, you will find them easier to undertake. A section on hand and machine appliqué is included in the book to help you.

Each finished block is 11" x 11". For each block, cut a 14" square, center your chosen flower block on the background square, and, after the appliqué is finished, you can re-cut the background square down to size or to the size you wish.

For each of the ten flowers in the book, you have a history and description of each flower, three full-sized patterns for each flower (single, multi-headed, and border design), an artist's impression of the flower, and some hints and tips on the appliqué techniques used, as many of the designs in this book have one pattern piece overlapping another. The designs have numbers shown on them — these are the order in which you sew the pieces. On the multi-flower blocks, each flower is made in the same order.

I have used 100% cotton fabric throughout for the background. This can be plain, have a small-scale print, or be mottled, but a lighter background complements the flowers the best. The flowers have been completed using plain and mottled fabrics, which allow your flowers to come alive. The blocks in the photographs have been completed by using both hand and machine appliqué methods and 100% cotton threads.

Appliqué Basics

Appliqué is attaching one or more fabrics to the background fabric with hand or machine stitching; it is always a good idea to lay the appliqué pieces out on your background fabric before starting to sew. This enables you to check your color choices and placement of the pieces and the overlaps. I suggest lightly marking the front of the background fabric to help with positioning the pieces, but be sure to avoid using water-soluble markers as the heat from your iron may cause the lines to become permanent. Always use a matching thread when sewing by hand or machine unless you wish to have a contrast effect.

1. Hand Appliqué Needle-turning Method

The fabric for hand appliqué is cut a scant 1/4" larger than the pattern piece. Clip all inside curves to within a couple of threads of the finished size — the tighter the curve, the more clips that are required. Outside curves are not clipped. For points, fold under the left side first and then the right, pin in place, and slip stitch down, using your needle to turn under the seam allowance as you sew.

2. Freezer Paper Appliqué

Cut the freezer paper to the exact size of the appliqué pieces required and press the shiny side of the freezer paper to the wrong side of the fabric. Cut out, adding a scant 1/4" seam allowance. Press the seam allowance over the freezer paper to give a crisp edge and pin in position on the background fabric. Slip stitch around the shape, leaving a small gap to allow you to remove the freezer paper before completing your stitching.

3. Machine Appliqué

For machine appliqué, use a sewing machine with a neat, close zigzag or blanket stitch. A blanket stitch is less dense than a zigzag stitch and can eliminate the use of a stabilizer at the back of your work. Always check your tensions, both upper and lower, and alter your stitch length to suit your choice of stitch.

Apply a fusible web to the back of your fabric and then cut out each drawn shape; you do not need to add a seam allowance. Press each shape into position and, using a zigzag stitch, satin stitch or buttonhole stitch machine around each piece.

4. Finishing

If you are going to hand quilt your work, it would be easier to sew through as few layers as possible. You may wish to cut away some of the background fabric or stabilizer used behind the appliqué, cutting approximately 3/16" from the sewing line, taking care not to cut any stitches or appliqué fabrics.

Single Flower Wall-Hanging

Multi-Headed Flower Wall-Hanging

Arum Lilly or Cala Lily

And the stately lilies stand
Fair in silvery light
Like saintly vestals, pale in prayer;
Their pure breath sanctifies the air
As its fragrance fills the night air

~ *Anonymous*

The main and most significant meaning is "magnificence" and "beauty." The name finds its origin from a Greek word for beauty. In Greek mythology, the lily was dedicated to the goddess Hera, the wife of Zeus. Hera, in a drugged sleep, breast-fed Alceme, born to a moral woman. When she awoke, Hera flung the baby away, and some of her milk flowed out and formed the Milky Way. It fell to earth, and thus, sprang the first lilies.

Another legend tells that the lily sprang from Eve's tears when she left the Garden of Eden. The lily was to Christians a symbol of pureness, chastity, and virtue and became closely associated with the Virgin Mary and later the symbol of virgin martyrs and many saints. The lily is also closely associated with the Resurrection and Easter. Throughout history, the Calla Lily has been expressed in art and paintings with the Virgin Mary or with the Angel of Annunciation. This is because it symbolizes purity, holiness, and faith.

The Arum Lily is the epitome of garden lilies having large white spathes, five to nine inches long, surrounding a conspicuous yellow spadix with leaves mid to deep green, slightly glossy, and arrow-shaped.

Arum Lily Single Flower

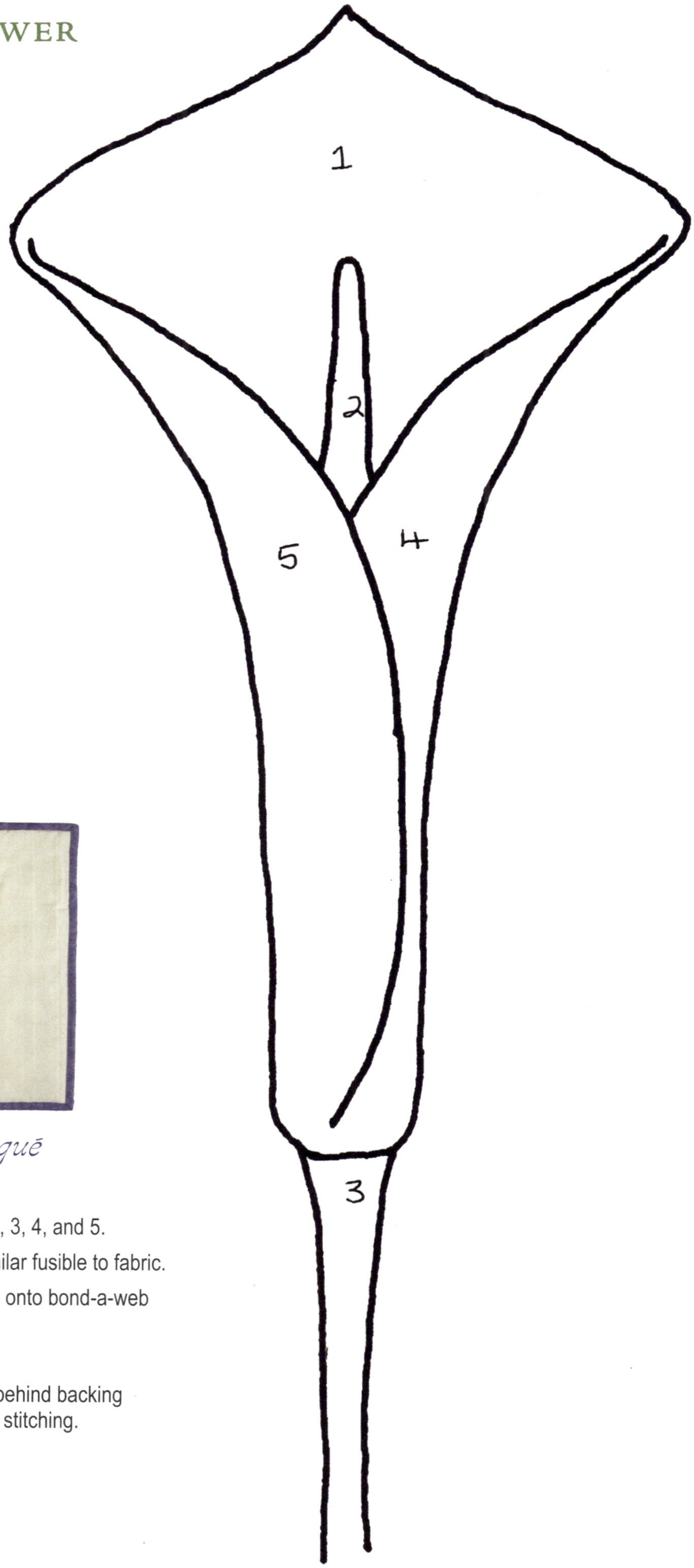

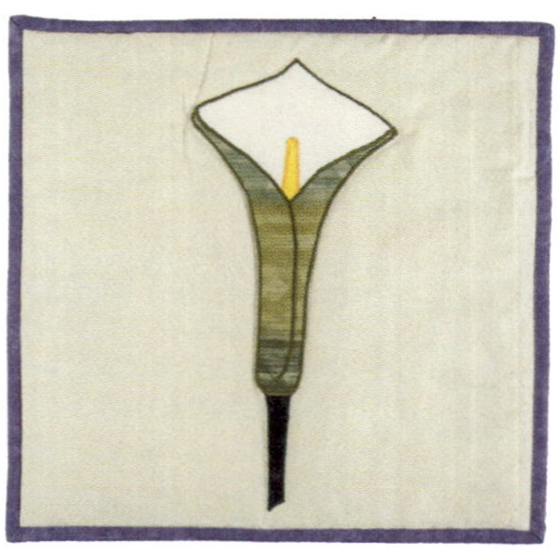

Machine Appliqué Hints & Tips

- Make templates for 1, 2, 3, 4, and 5.
- Affix Bond-a-web or similar fusible to fabric.
- Trace around templates onto bond-a-web and cut out pieces.
- Iron pieces onto fabric.
- *Optional*: Place muslin behind backing to stabilize the machine stitching.

Arum Lily Multi Flower

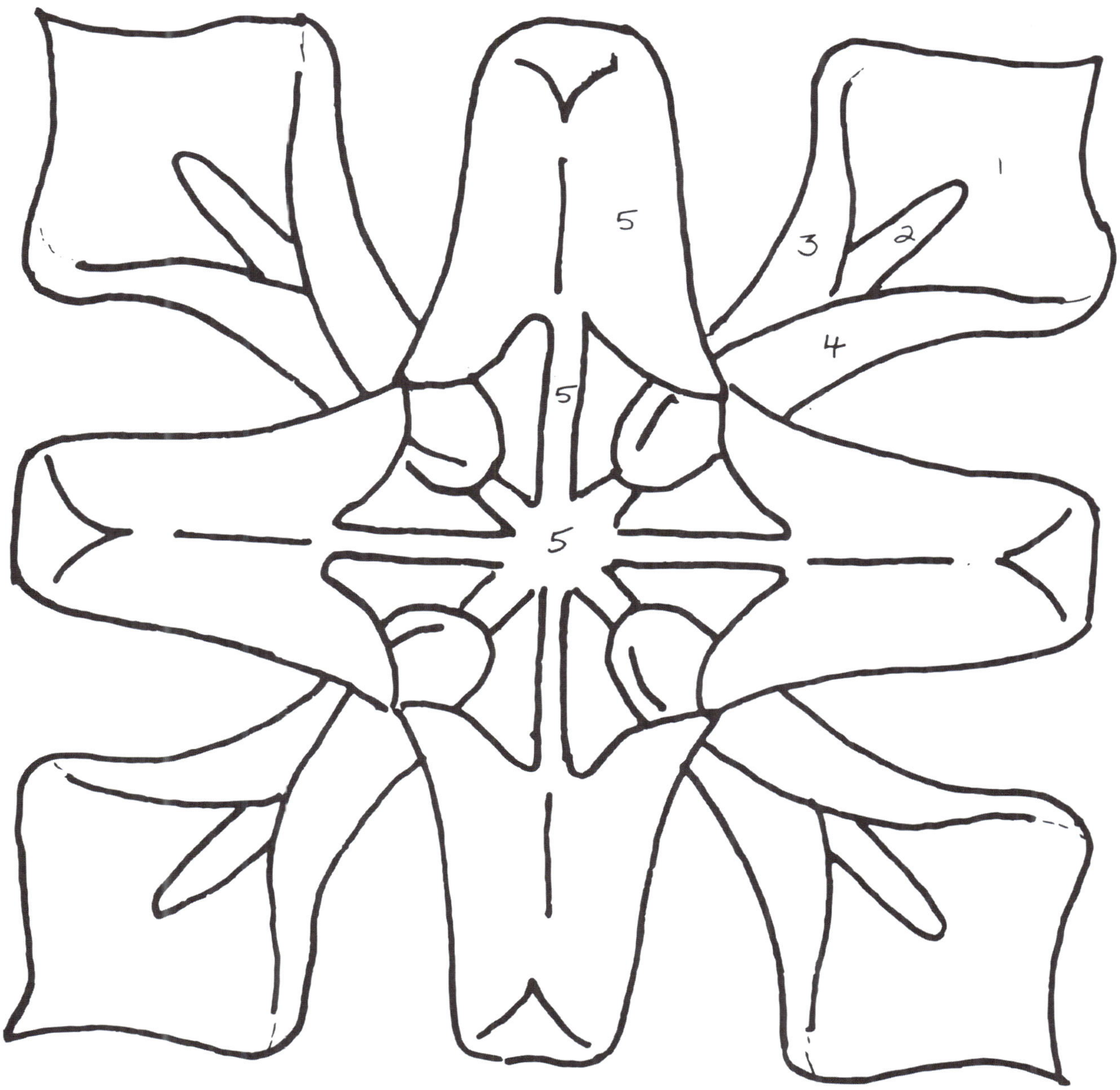

Hand Appliqué Hints & Tips

- Cut the leaves and stems (pieces marked "5") as one piece and then position on the background fabric, but stitch down only the center "X" stem. Leave remaining part unattached.
- Position the four flowers and stitch as numbered (pieces marked 1 to 4).
- Position the four leaves and long stems that you left unattached and stitch in place.
- Machine embellish.

Arum Lily Border

Hand Appliqué Hints & Tips

With this block, you may choose to alter the design (as in the picture of the finished border blocks top) by removing the flowers/leaves at one end of the design and adding to the other end to make three complete flowers and three leaves.

- Using freezer paper, the needle turned method may help with the smaller pieces (marked 1 and 2).
- Cut piece marked "5" as a whole and place under piece marked "6." This allows piece marked "7" to go on top.
- Work this block in order, i.e. all 1s and then 2s, etc.

Celandine

I'll befall the yellow flowers,
Children of the flaring hours!
Buttercups, that will be seen,
Whether we will see or no;
Others, too, of lofty mien,
They have done as worldlings do;
Taken praise that should be thine,
Little, humble Celandine!

~ *William Wordsworth*

Tradition has it that the Celandine name derives from the Greek *chelidon* (a swallow), because it comes into flower when the swallows arrive and fades at their departure. (The English name Celandine is merely a corruption of the Greek word.)

The fair maids of France and Kent sought the double variety of white bachelor's buttons, as they were known.

A colony of monks who lived on Steepholm, in the Bristol Channel between 1166 and 1260, were recorded as using Steepholms' equitable oceanic climate for the growing of Mediterranean herbs, including the Celandine. In the Middle Ages, the Celandine was used as a drug plant and was supposed to be good for the blood. Clusius, the celebrated Dutch botanist, considered the juice, dropped into small green wounds, effected rapid cure and, when dropped into the eye, would take away specks and stop incipient suffusions. The old alchemists held that it was good to "super-stifle the jaundice," because of its intense yellow color.

The Celandine is one of the year's first flowers to bloom in the United Kingdom, sometimes appearing as early as February. The golden blooms of Celandine, shining like tiny suns in the darkening grass, are a sign that spring has arrived.

Celandine leaves are a shiny, dark green, sometimes mottled with purple. The flowers are solitary, long-stalked, with greenish sepals and shiny yellow petals often streaked with purple on the outside. The Celandine can present itself in all shades, from pale straw to the golden crocus; the yellow fading to white, tints of red, pink, rose, and flame colored.

Celandine Single Flower

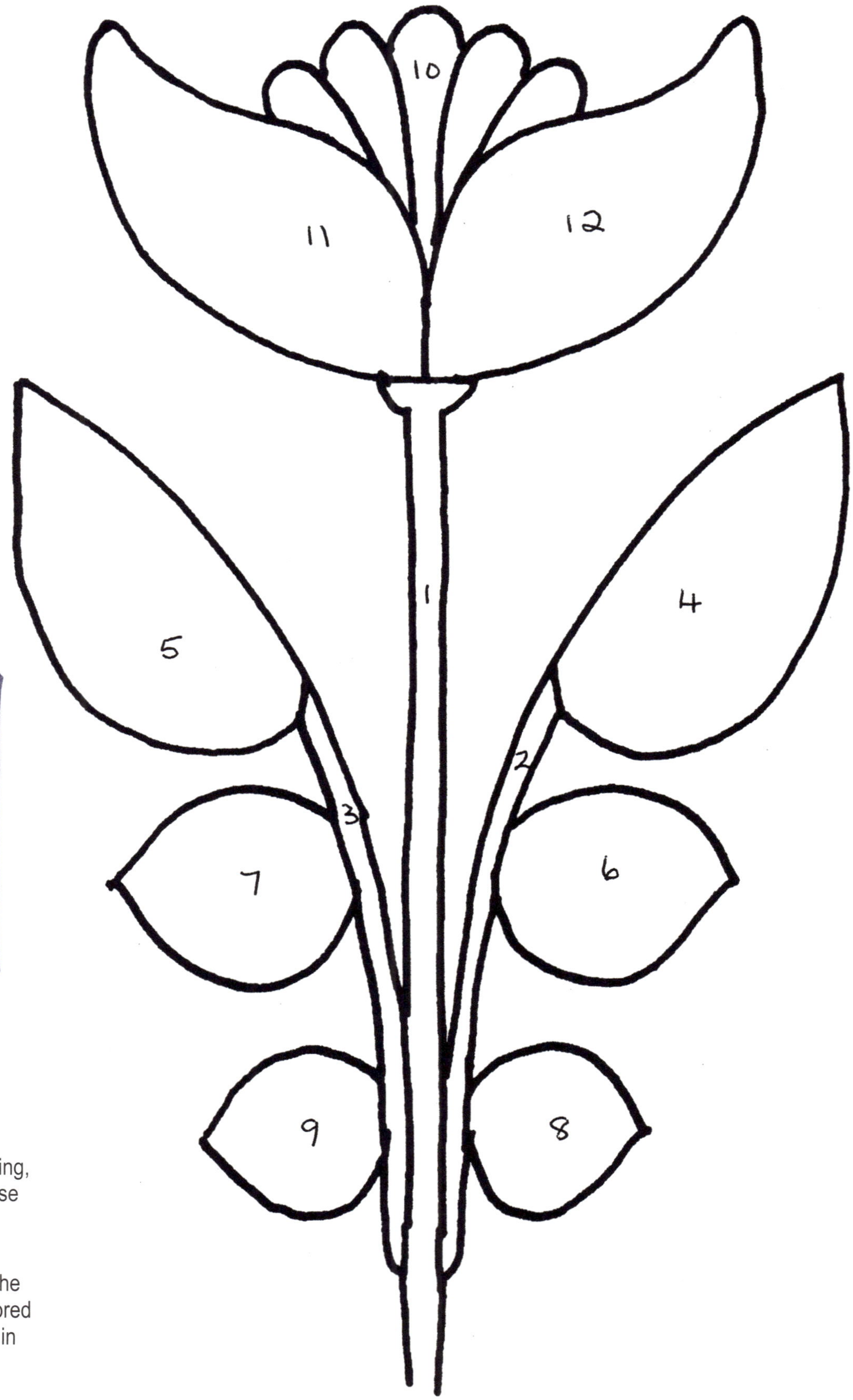

Machine Appliqué Hints & Tips

- Apply pieces using Heat'n'Bond or similar
- To stop the satin stitch from puckering, use a stabilizing fabric on the reverse side of the background fabric.
- Outline with satin stitch, using free motion embroidery, and embellish the leaves and flower using similar colored embroidery thread and gold thread in the center.

Celandine Multi Flower

Hand Appliqué Hints & Tips

Optional: To make an easier block, exclude the center "garland" of oval leaves and the outer "garland" of round leaves.

- Using freezer paper, cut the stems (piece marked 1) and the leaves (piece marked 2) as one complete piece.
- Cut the three sections that make the top part of the flowers as one piece and machine embellish to highlight them as the four parts of the flower head.

Celandine Border

Machine Appliqué Hints & Tips

- Pieces applied using Heat'n'Bond or similar.
- Machine stitch using satin stitch.
- Border and leaf section (marked "6") can be sewn as a complete piece.

Convolvulus
(Dwarf Morning Glory)

Bring hither the pink and purple Columbine with Gillyflower;
Bring Columbine and Sops in wine,
Worn of paramours.
Strew the ground with Daffadowndillies,
And Cowslips, and Kingcups,
And loved Lilies;
The pretty Pawnce, and the Cherisaunce,
Shall match with the fair flower Delice.

~ *Herbert Spencer*

In Casa del Bracciale d'Oro, at Pompeii, preserved under volcanic ash since AD 79, a garden scene painted on walls included twining convolvulus with pink and white lilies. The *Horti Farnesiani* laid out by Vignola in the mid-sixteenth century included *convolvulus* from Peru.

In Ancient Egypt, the leaves and flowers were often part of wreaths and garlands, but they were also among the plants to be offered to the gods on their own.

In religious circles, it is known as "Ladies Nightcap" or "Ladies Mantle."

The *Convolvulus* has freely-branching reddish stems that are thin and threadlike. Each flower is a wide-mouthed trumpet, usually a clear blue/mauve or ultramarine in color, with white and golden yellow hearts and throats in the center and the underside having mauve strips. Several varieties are found, ranging from dark blue to pastel pinks and mauves, as well as the brilliant blues. Wild convolvulus ranges from white to pink, to pink with white strips and white with pink strips to a yellowish color.

Convolvulus Single Flower

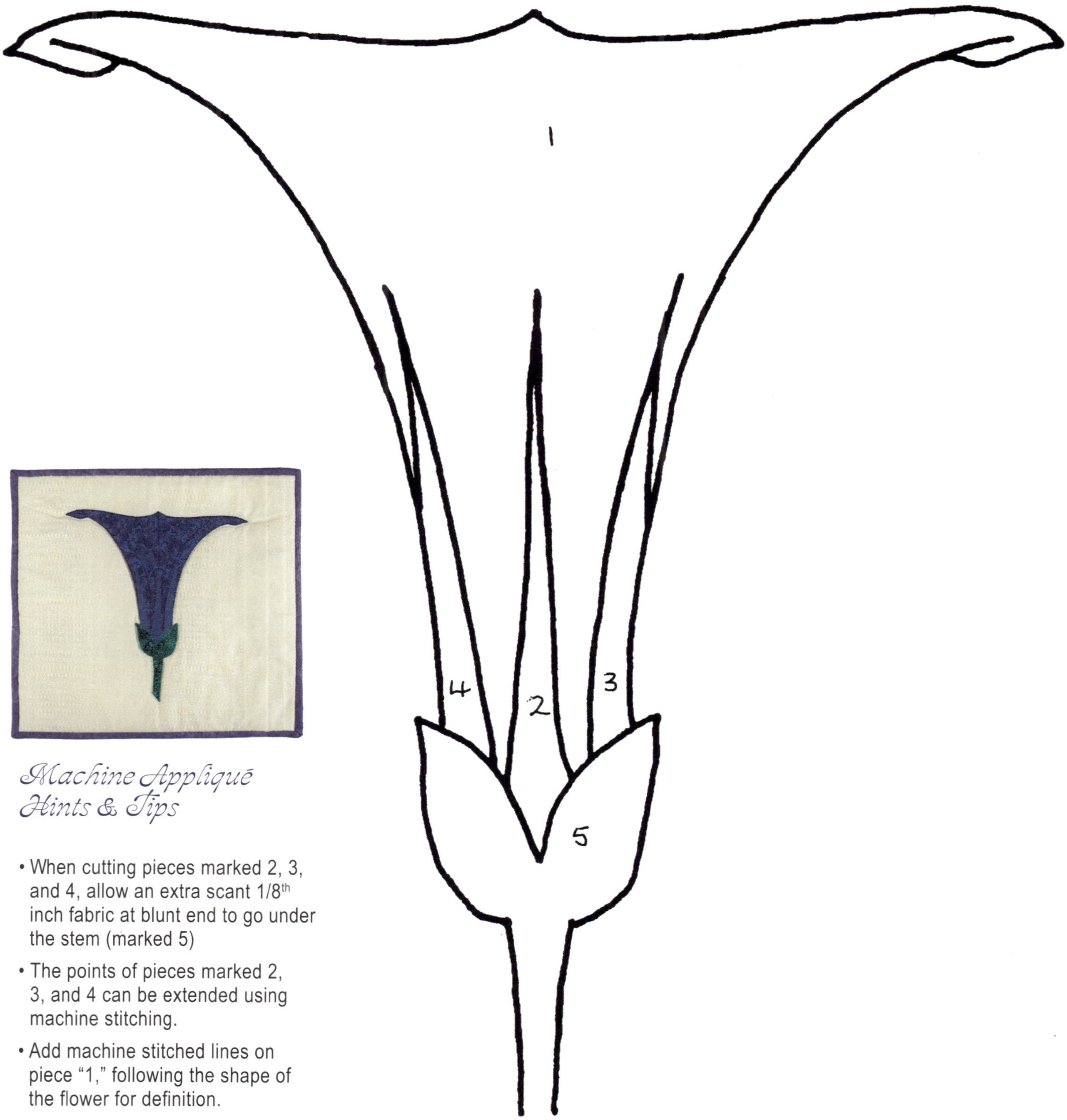

Machine Appliqué Hints & Tips

- When cutting pieces marked 2, 3, and 4, allow an extra scant 1/8th inch fabric at blunt end to go under the stem (marked 5)
- The points of pieces marked 2, 3, and 4 can be extended using machine stitching.
- Add machine stitched lines on piece "1," following the shape of the flower for definition.

Convolvulus Multi Flower

Hand Appliqué Hints & Tips

- Using freezer paper, appliqué and cut the leaves, stems, and flower bases as one piece (marked "3").
- The elongated "dagger" on the petal (marked "2") can be formed by machine stitching or cutting a shape and extending it with machine stitching.
- Embellish with machine stitching to form veins on the leaves and folds on the flowers.

Convolvulus Border

Hand Appliqué Hints & Tips

- For piece marked "1", cut strip 1/2 inch wide. (The bottom border line is optional.)
- Cut out pieces marked 2 and 3 as one piece in the main flower color.
- Cut out and stitch the piece marked 3 (lighter color) on top of piece 2.
- Cut piece marked 4 slightly longer to allow for going under piece marked 5.
- Machine embellished to define folds in the petals.

Crocus

In blue and yellow from its grave
Springs up the crocus fair,
And God shall raise those bright blue eyes,
Those sunny waves of hair.
Not for a fading summer's morn,
Not for a fleeting hour,
But for an endless age of bliss,
Shall rise our heart's dear flower

~ *Harriet Beecher Stowe*

The origin of the species is lost in antiquity, but the people best known as growers of this bulb were the Minoans. These people traded saffron throughout the eastern 3/4 of the Mediterranean, and they had done it since 1550 BC at the latest, as a fresco on the Island of Santorini (modern Thira) just north of Crete shows women collecting the crocus for the saffron crop.

By the time of Pliny the Elder (1 AD), it had become an important crop on Sicily. How the crocus came to England is lost in the veil of history. Some historians say that one of the bulbs was brought by the Romans to England; another that the crocus was smuggled inside a hollowed out staff by an Algerian pilgrim at the time of the Crusades, but it was possibly the autumn-flowering *crocus sativus* that arrived first.

The crocus is thought of in the United Kingdom as a spring flower and its arrival is patiently awaited throughout the winter months. It has also long been associated with Valentines Day (February 14th).

Crocus blooms can be yellow, purple with lilac inners, and white with stocals of purple or lilac, lilac pink, or blue in color with orange styles. The leaves are linear, grooved green with a white midriff.

Crocus
Single Flower

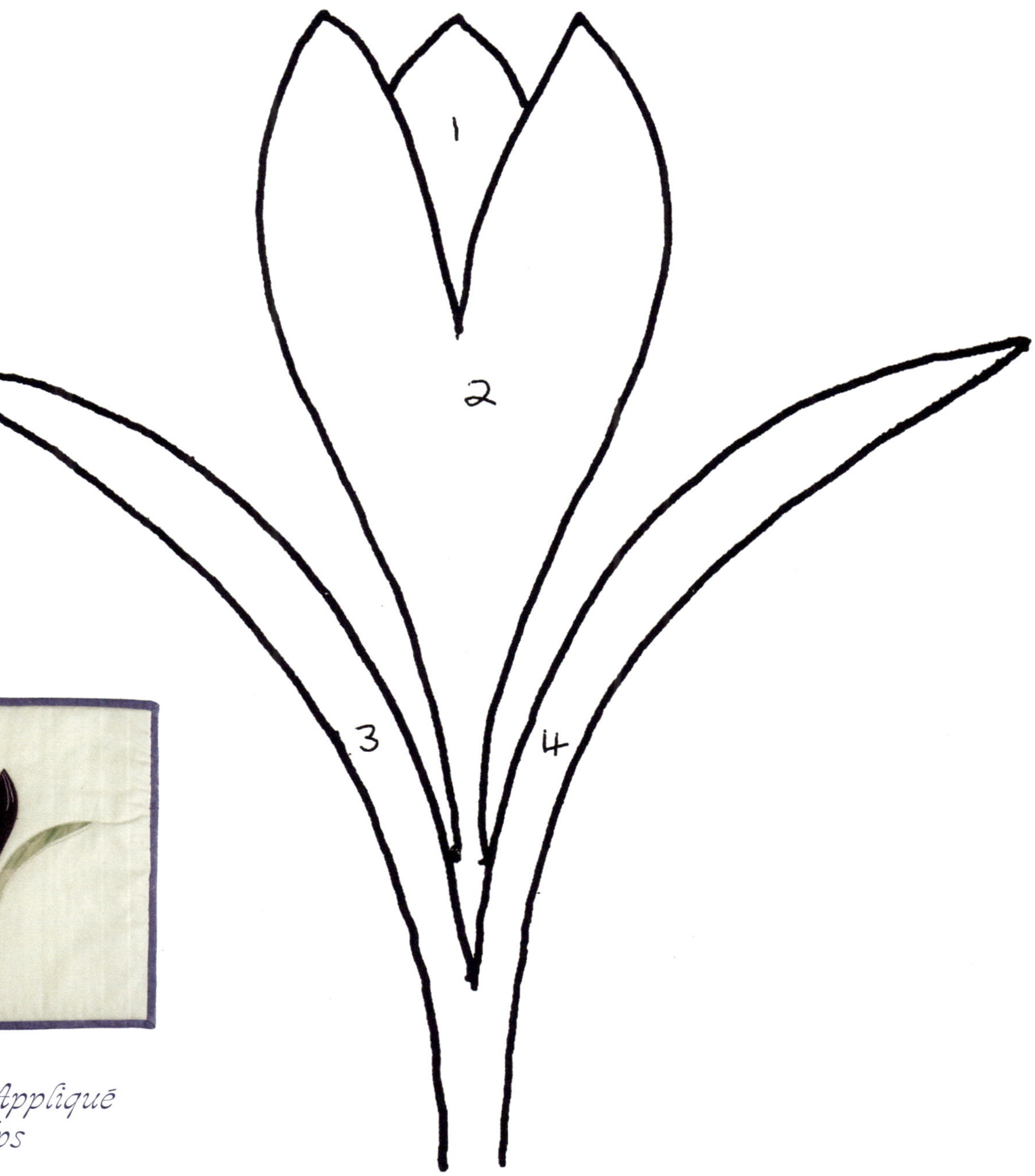

Machine Appliqué Hints & Tips

- Add an extra 1/8 inch on the bottom end of the pieces marked 1, 2, and 3, as these go under other pieces.
- If using one fabric color for the flower, it can be cut as one piece (pieces marked 1 and 2) and machine embellished to define the petals.
- If a contrast is required, use two fabrics and cut the two pieces marked 1 and 2 separately.

Crocus
Multi Flower

Hand Appliqué Hints & Tips

- The leaves pieces marked 5 and 6 can be cut in pairs rather than individually.
- The center "cross" (marked "1") can be cut as one piece rather than four individual pieces and also reduced. Use machine stitching to define the tips.
- The petals (marked 2, 3, and 4) can be cut as one complete piece rather than individually and then machine embellished to define the separate petals.

Crocus Border

Machine Appliqué Hints & Tips

- The top border can be omitted and the bottom border (piece marked 4) can be finished at 1/2 inch wide.
- The flowers can be cut as one piece or two, as shown on the design (pieces marked 1 and 2).
- This block can be completed by using heat 'n' bond or similar.
- To fit three flowers into the border block, overlap the leaves when positioning and use two different green fabrics on the alternating leaves.

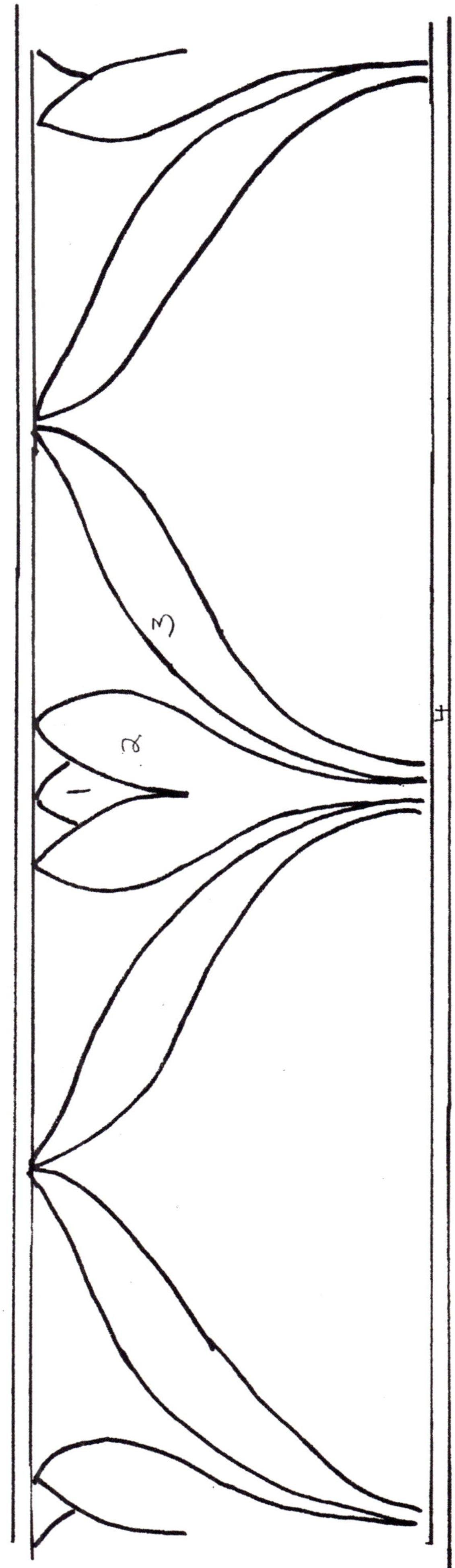

Dog Rose (Fruit)

"If I should never taste the salt sea spray
As the ship beats her course across the breeze.
Or smell the dog-rose and new-mown hay,
or moss or primroses beneath the tree."

~ *Major Malcolm Boyd, killed in action in France, June 1944*

Evidence of Dog Rose hips has been recorded in and around ancient settlements, suggesting that the shrub has a long association with mankind. One theory is that the ancient Greeks may have just been denigrating the worth of Dog Rose as a garden plant by using the belittling term "dog." The Romans believed it was to cure the bite of a mad dog, so the name is a reference to the medieval Latin Rosa Canina, stemming from the ancient Latin (originally Greek) word *cynorrhodon*. The hips of the Dog Rose were a popular sweetmeat in the Middle Ages. The plants were not esteemed to the same degree as were cultivated roses (see *R. gallica*, following entry), but Dog Rose was valued as the source of a widely-used folk remedy for chest problems

It has been printed that sixty years after the birth of Christ the first recorded treatment of rabies occurred. A Roman woman dreamed she was to send the roots of the rose to her son serving in the Roman army in Spain. Just before the package arrived, the soldier was bitten by a mad dog and contracted rabies, and a tea of the roots cured the disease.

In the United Kingdom, around Halloween and Thanksgiving, the urn-shaped, formerly hard, green and shiny fruit, called rose hips, gradually become soft, scarlet, and full of delicious pulp. As the leaves turn yellow and drop for winter, the hips make an attractive show. When ripe, the fruit are shiny-red, hairless, oval or rounded, and without sepals, with wide, often-raised disc, and narrow orifice

Dog Rose
Single Flower

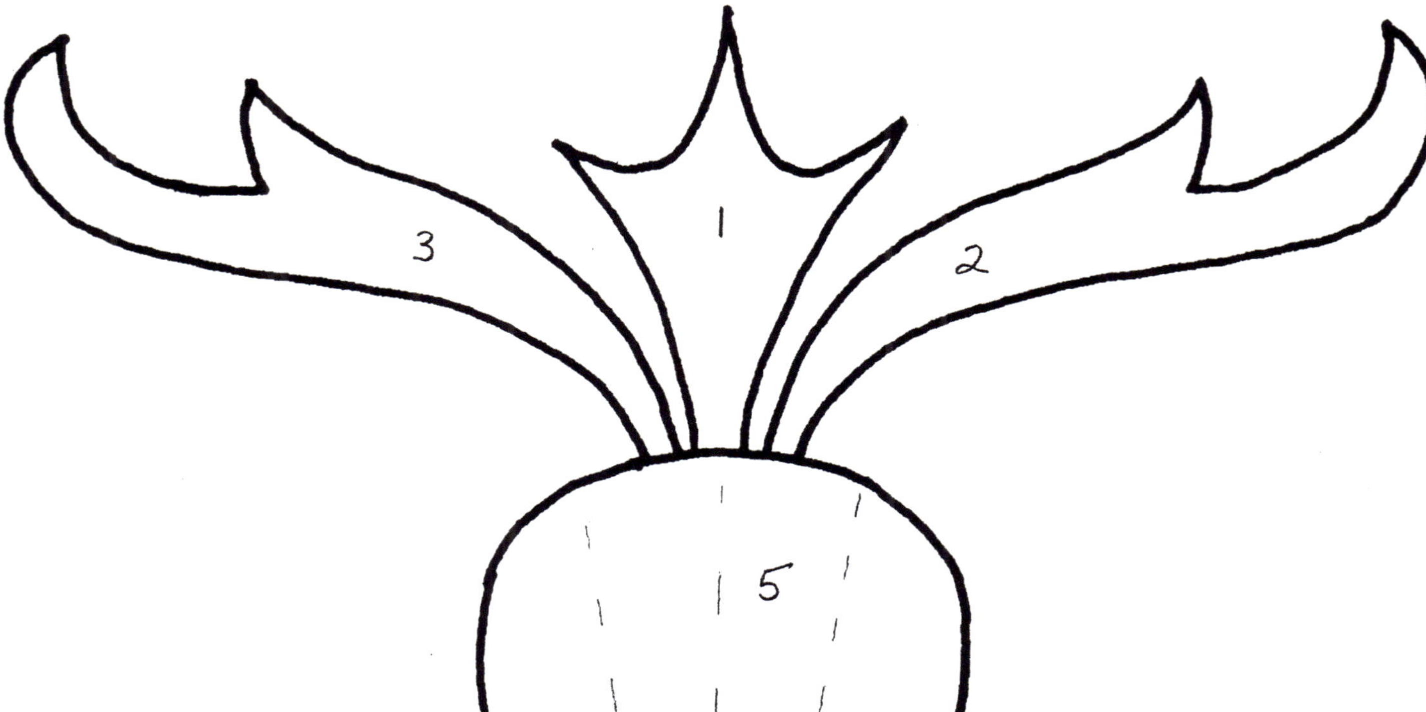

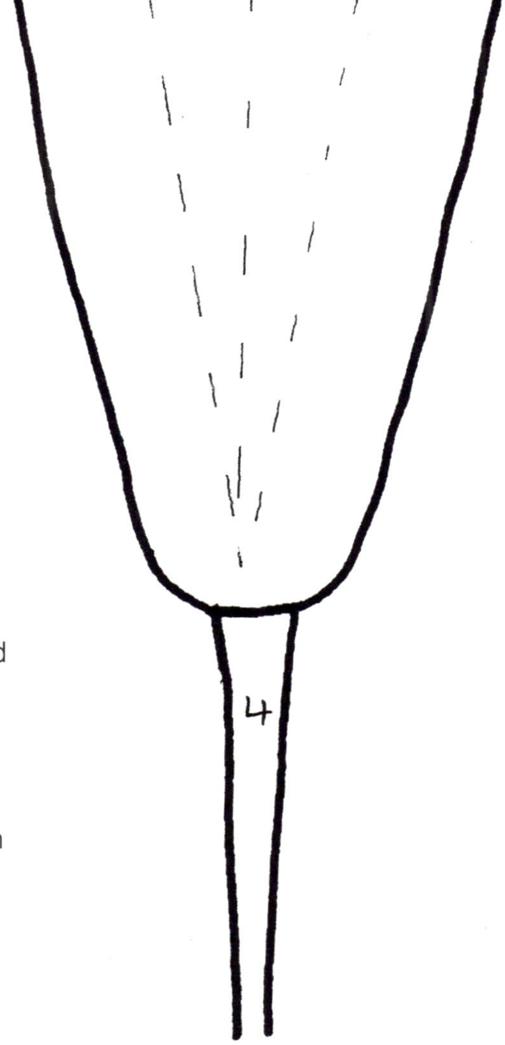

Machine Appliqué Hints & Tips

- Use Heat'n'Bond or similar.
- When cutting pieces marked 1, 2, 3, and 4, allow a scant extra 1/8 inch fabric on the bottom edge.
- Place pieces marked 1, 2, 3, and 4 under piece 5.
- These can be bonded together and then machine appliquéd.
- Embellish by machine straight stitching three lines on piece 5.

Hand Appliqué Hints & Tips

- This block was made by needle turned appliqué.
- The horned leaves on the center stem are optional; you can just use straight crossed stems to join the four (3-leaf) pieces.
- Cut the leaves and stem (marked 1) as one complete piece.
- Cut the "fruit" and "horns" (marked 2) as one piece rather than three separate pieces.
- Machine embellish to define the leaves and "horns."

Dog Rose Border

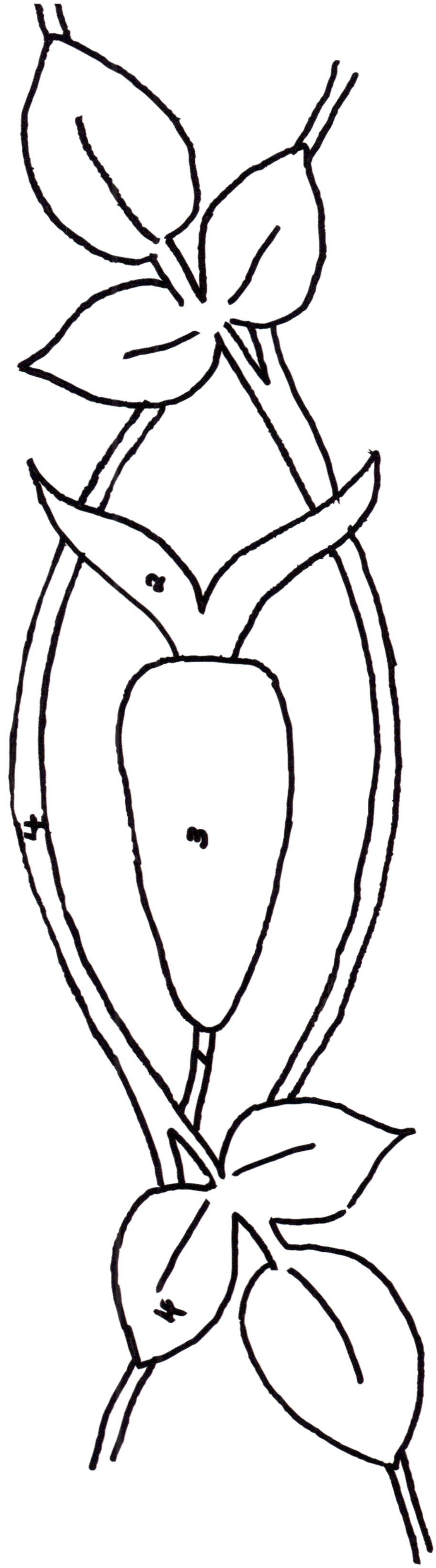

Machine Appliqué Hints & Tips

- Cut piece marked "1" a scant 1/8 inch longer at both ends for it to go under the pieces 3 and 4.
- Cut piece marked "2" a scant 1/8 inch longer to go under piece 3.
- Cut piece marked 4 out as a whole (you can add the leaves individually if you wish).
- Machine embellish to define the Dog Rose fruit and leaves.

Harebell

...On the windy hills
Lo, the little harebell leans
On the spire-grass that it queens
With bonnets blue.

v~ George Meredith

According to folklore, the Harebell is the flower of witches and the witches gave it names such as witches' thimbles, fairy bells, and old man's bells, the old man being the devil. Witches are said to have used its juice as part of flying ointment. The Harebell is also thought to be unlucky, especially if it is brought into the home. The Harebell was the "fairy plant" of southwest England; in the Isle of Man the "fairies thimble" and the "bluebell" of Scotland. The Harebell is also used in the garland ceremony at the Oxfordshire village of Bampton at Whitsuntide.

Christian lore associates the Harebell with the Virgin Mary, and the flower is dedicated in some Roman Catholic countries to St. Dominic (c.1170-1221), the patron saint of astronomers. The Harebell is associated in England with St. Georges Day (April 23rd) and is associated with humility and grief.

The Harebell flowers, which hang on fine stems and nod their delicate blue bells in the breeze, can vary from blue to violet blue, lavender blue to violet, and light lavender to deep lavender blue. The dark green leaves are heart-shaped or rounded. The bells are formed of five petals joined at their edges. Five freestanding stamens surround a central style.

Harebell Single Flower

Machine Appliqué Hints & Tips

- The pieces marked 1 and 2 (flower petals) can be cut as one complete piece.
- Cut piece marked "3" a scant 1/8 inch longer on the end where it goes under piece 4.
- The leaves can also be cut as one large piece (marked 4, 5, 6, 7, and 8) rather than individual pieces — do not include pieces marked 9 and 10, as these are the reverse side of the leaves.
- If the leaves are cut as one piece, use machine stitching to embellish and define the edges of the individual leaves.
- Beads can be used to embellish the block (see block colored picture).

Harebell Multi Flower

Hand Appliqué Hints & Tips

- The leaves can be cut as a whole piece rather than individually, except the pieces marked “2” — these need to be cut separately as they are the reverse side of the leaves and use a different color of green.
- The tulip flowers can also be cut as one piece (marked 4, 5, and 6) and then machine embellished to define the separate petals.
- Cut piece marked “3” a scant 1/8 inch longer where it goes under the piece marked “1”.

Harebell Border

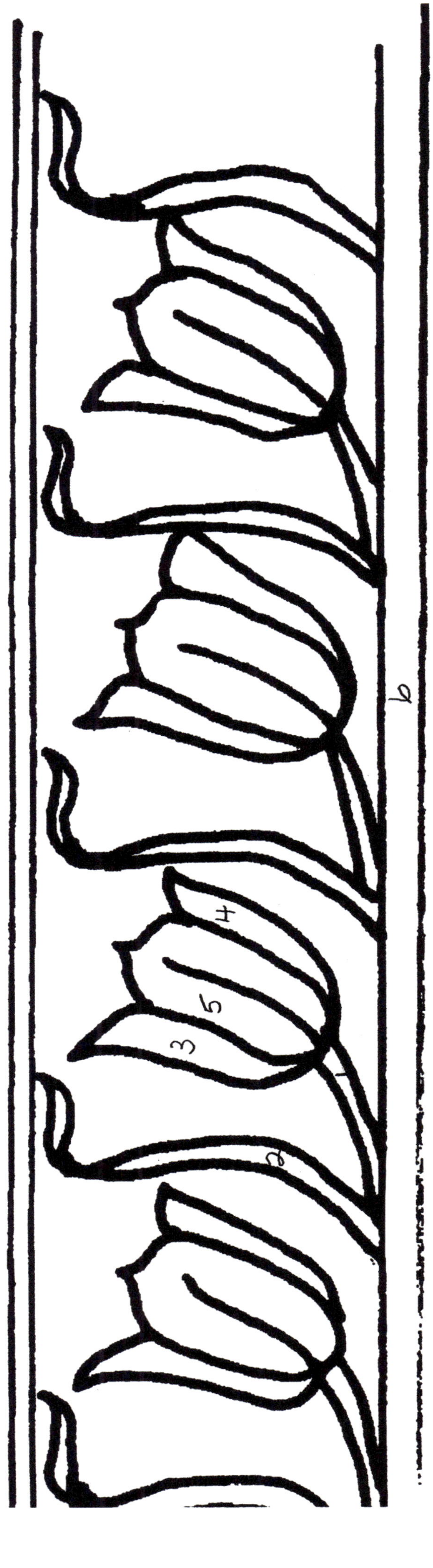

Machine Appliqué Hints & Tips

- The top border can be omitted from the block.
- The bottom border (piece marked 6) can be made to 1/2" finished width.
- Each flower can be cut out as one piece rather than individual pieces (pieces marked 3, 4, and 5) and then machine embellished to define the different petals.
- Add an extra 1/8 inch to the lower edge of pieces marked 1 and 2, as these are placed under the piece marked 6.

Snowdrop

Brother, Joy to you
I've brought some snowdrops; only just a few,
But quite enough to prove the world awake,
Cheerful and hopeful in the frosty dew
And for the pale sun's sake.

~ *Christina Rosetti*

Some older English names for the Snowdrop were Fair Maids of February, Candlemas Bells, Mary's Taper, Snow Piercer, Dingle-Dangle, and White Ladies. All of these names came from its association with the Feast of the Purification of the Virgin Mary, or Candlemas Day on February 2nd, when it was custom that maidens dressed in white, should carry snowdrops to church, and strew them on the alter. The Snowdrop has long been considered a sacred plant, particularly to virgins. A holy symbol of chastity and purity, it was often found in convent gardens, but it was also found on monastic sites and churchyards across Britain. Monks dedicated the white flowers to the Virgin Mary as snowdrops bloomed at the time she took the child Jesus to the Temple.

The Victorians considered the Snowdrop a death token, likening the outer petals to a shroud. To them, the closeness of the flowers to the earth meant that the flower belonged more to the dead than the living. It was regarded as unlucky to bring the flower into the house, despite it being a symbol of Candlemas.

The flowers are white with green-tipped inner segments, a yellow-green cap, and pale green leaves.

Snowdrop Single Flower

Hand Appliqué Hints & Tips

The snowdrop can look very pale and delicate against the other blocks. Make sure your green fabric is a good green and contrasts well to the white and paler green fabrics used in the rest of the flower.

- Cut pieces marked 1, 2, 3, and 6 a scant 1/8 inch longer where they go under other pieces.
- Use embellishments to make the snowdrop stand out and to add definition to the leaves and flower.

Snowdrop Multi Flower

Hand Appliqué Hints & Tips

- Use a very lightweight iron-on Vilene to stabilize the fabric.
- Cut all the leaf pieces marked "1" as one complete piece.
- The stems marked piece "2" can be formed by stitching a narrow tube; trim and press the seam edge underneath and then stitch them down over the center X of piece "1" and under piece "6."
- When applying piece "6" at the base of the petals, use a small gathering stitch around the curves to help keep the piece flat when stitching.

Snowdrop Border

Machine Appliqué Hints & Tips

- The border strips are optional.
- Cut out and place on your background fabric all the pieces. Each piece can then be sewn in order or you can complete one flower at a time. Be sure that your placement is correctly marked.
- Allow a scant 1/8" additional length on pieces 1, 2, 3, 4, and 5 where they go under one of the other pieces. The same applies to the piece marked "7."

Tulip

Those tulips that such wealth display,
To court my eye, shall loose their name,
Though now they listen, as if they
Expected I should praise their flame.

~ *James Shirley*

Turks wore the tulip bloom in their turbans and the name is thought to be a corruption of the word "tulipant." Tulips can be traced back to the middle of the sixteenth century, but it is believed that tulips may have been grown either as wild or cultivated plants in the gardens of the King Tiglath-Pileser I (1114–1026 BC). The tulip's popularity as a flower is documented in the next century as "tulipmania." Tales of fantastic prices for a single bulb in Dutch auction rooms expound.

According to Persian legend, the first tulips sprung up from the bloodshed by a lover and for a long time the tulip was the symbol of avowed love. Another legend recounts that a Persian youth, rejected by a maiden, died of a broken heart in the desert and his tears, as they fell into the sand, turned into a beautiful tulip.

In Christianity, the tulip, known as Mary's Prayer, was said to represent Mary's fullness of grace. Its upward-facing cup or chalice reflected Our Lady's openness to and filling with grace.

The Tulip's colors can range from white through various yellows, pinks, and reds to dark purple. An almost black has also been raised. The leaves are linear, grass-like, and greyish green, with the upper surface channelled.

Tulip
Single Flower

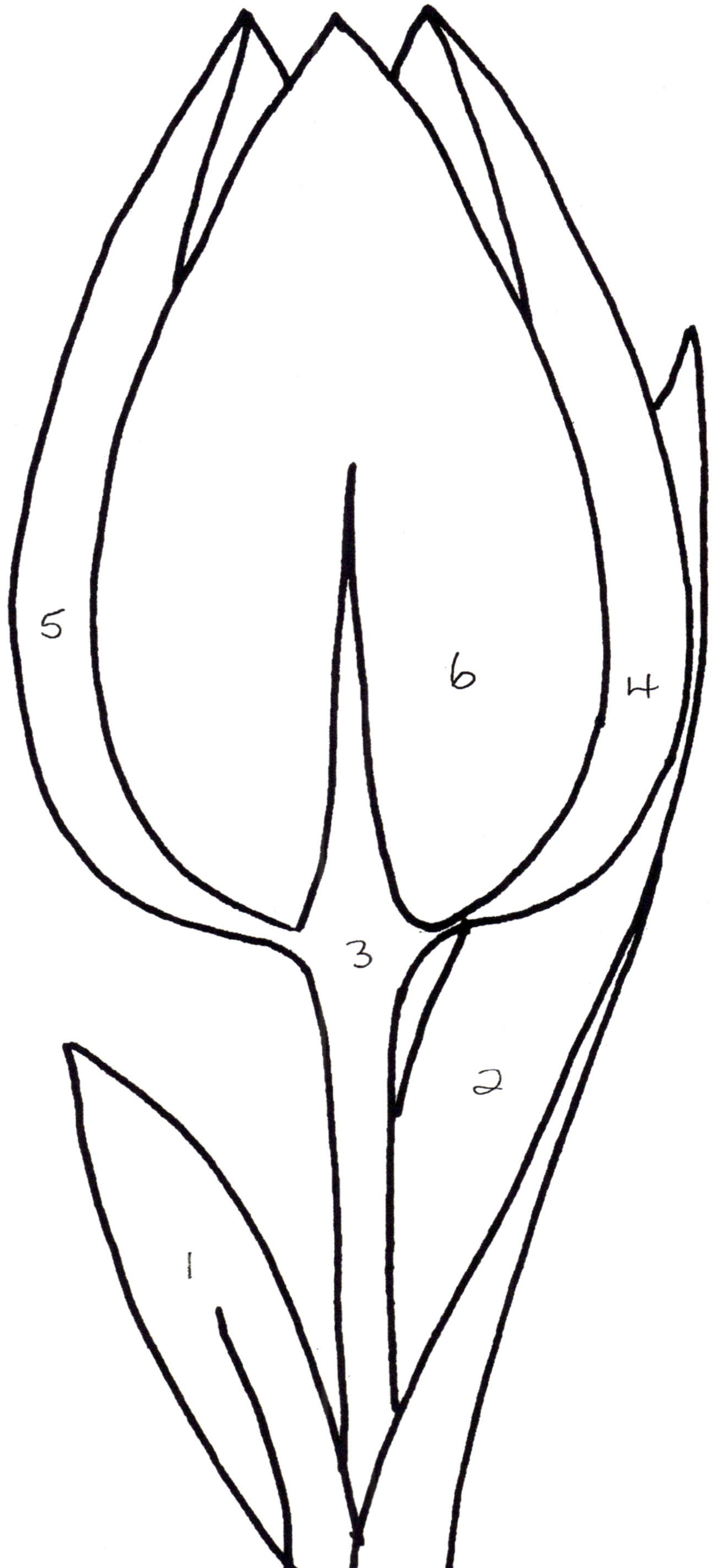

Machine Appliqué Hints & Tips

- Cut the piece marked "2" as a complete leaf and use machine stitching to emphasize the fold on the leaf — this allows it to be placed under the tulip flower (pieces marked 4 and 6).
- The pieces marked "4," "5," and "6" can be cut as one complete flower and machine embellished to define the separate petals or the piece marked "6" can be cut as a separate piece and appliquéd on top of pieces "4" and "5" — this will give a raised effect to the flower.
- The point on piece "3" can be extended by machine stitching.

Tulip Multi Flower

Hand Appliqué Hints & Tips

- This block allows the background fabric to show through the center (like a cross).
- The tulip petals (pieces marked "3," "4," and "5") can be cut as one complete flower. When applied, they can be machine embellished to define them.
- Add an extra scant 1/8 inch to one end of the piece marked "2" as it goes under the flower pieces.

Tulip Border

Hand Appliqué Hints & Tips

- Using freezer paper helps with the construction of this block.
- Add a scant 1/8 inch extra to both ends of the piece marked "1" as it goes under the flower and piece 7.
- The tulip petals (pieces 2, 3, and 4) can be cut as one complete flower. When applied, they can be machine embellished to define them.
- If constructing the flower separately, begin by stitching the stem (piece 1) and the middle petal (piece 2) and then the two remaining petals, overlapping one petal at the center join (pieces 3 and 4).
- Stitch the two leaves in place (pieces 5 and 6).
- The bottom border strip (piece 7) can be finished 1/2" wide.

Water Lily

Now folds the lily all her sweetness up,
And slips into the bosom of the lake:
So fold thyself, my dearest thou, and slip
Into my bosom and be lost in me.

~ *Alfred, Lord Tennyson*

In pictures of the Annunciation, where Gabriel the Archangel appears to the Virgin Mary, he is holding in his hand a spray of water lilies — this spray typifies fire and water or the idea of creation and generation. The Water Lily symbolized Upper Egypt and was used, along with the papyrus flower that symbolized Lower Egypt, to depict a united country. The blue Water Lily was sacred to the Egyptians to whom it represented the sun and rebirth. During Tutankhamen's reign, the white Water Lily was the symbol of the god Osiris and was portrayed on mosaics as having rounded petals and sharply toothed leaves; the white flower does not open until mid-day and then retires in early evening.

The Water Lily is the first flower mentioned in world literature. In Asia, the flowering Water Lily, called the lotus, symbolizes absolute truth and purity. The bloom became associated with Buddha himself. The Hindus in India believe that, before its creation as we know it, the world was a golden lotus.

In Cheshire, the white variety is known locally as the "Lady of the Lake."

The most common feature of water lilies is their dark green circular leaves, which are wine-colored beneath. The flowers can range from white to pink and rose colored to crimson, red, yellow, or copper. The pure white semi-double variety has bright gold stamens. The flowers, large, showy, and fragrant, are often 6" in diameter.

Water Lily Single Flower

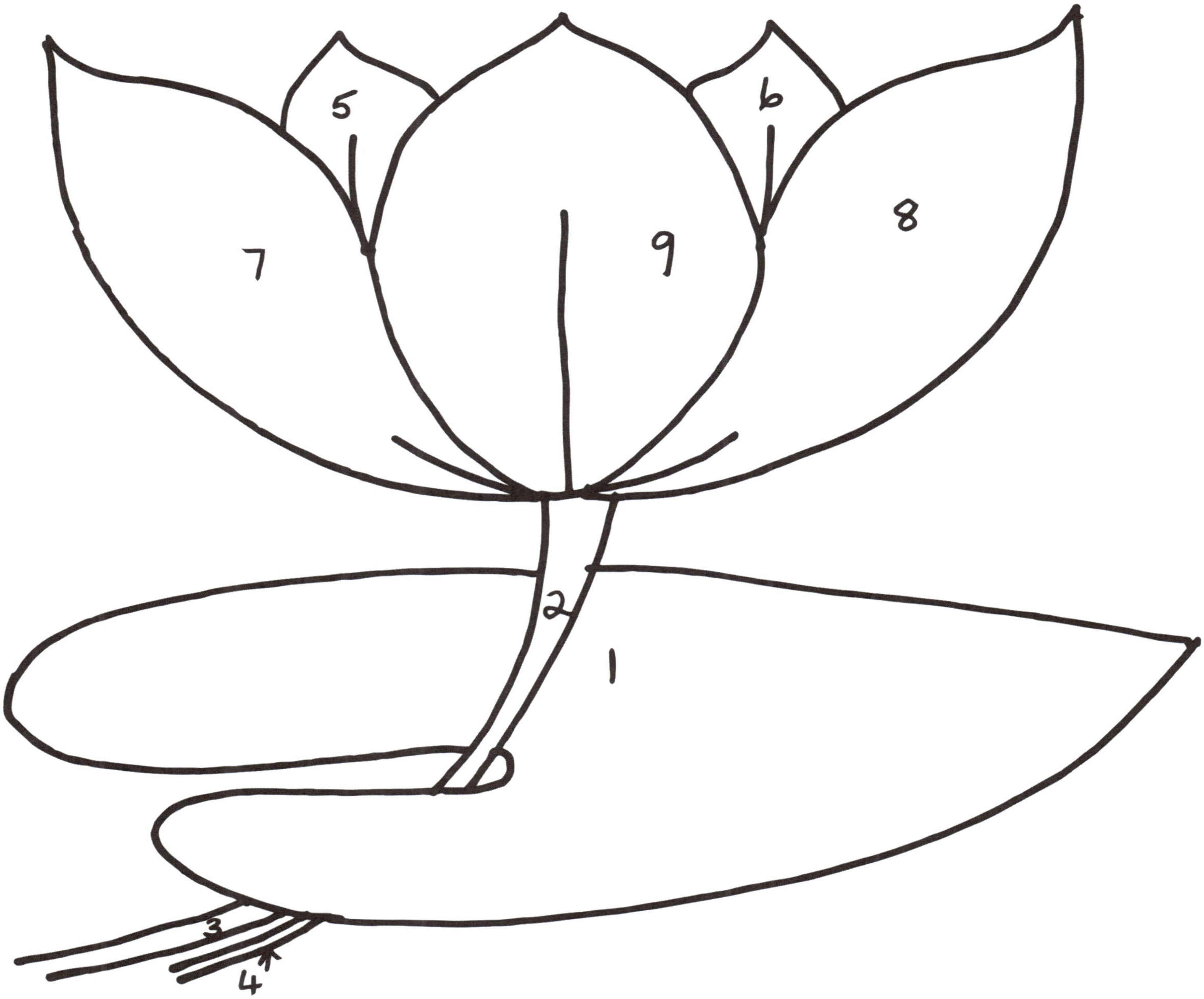

Machine Appliqué Hints & Tips

- Add a scant 1/8 inch to the top of the piece marked "2" as it goes under the flower.
- Cut the Lily leaf (piece marked 1) as a whole (not in two sections), then place the piece marked "4" over top piece 1 through "the gap." Be careful to allow for this when stitching.
- Add soft iron-on Vilene to the reverse of the block to help with stability.
- Use machine stitches to embellish and define the petals.

Water Lily
Multi Flower

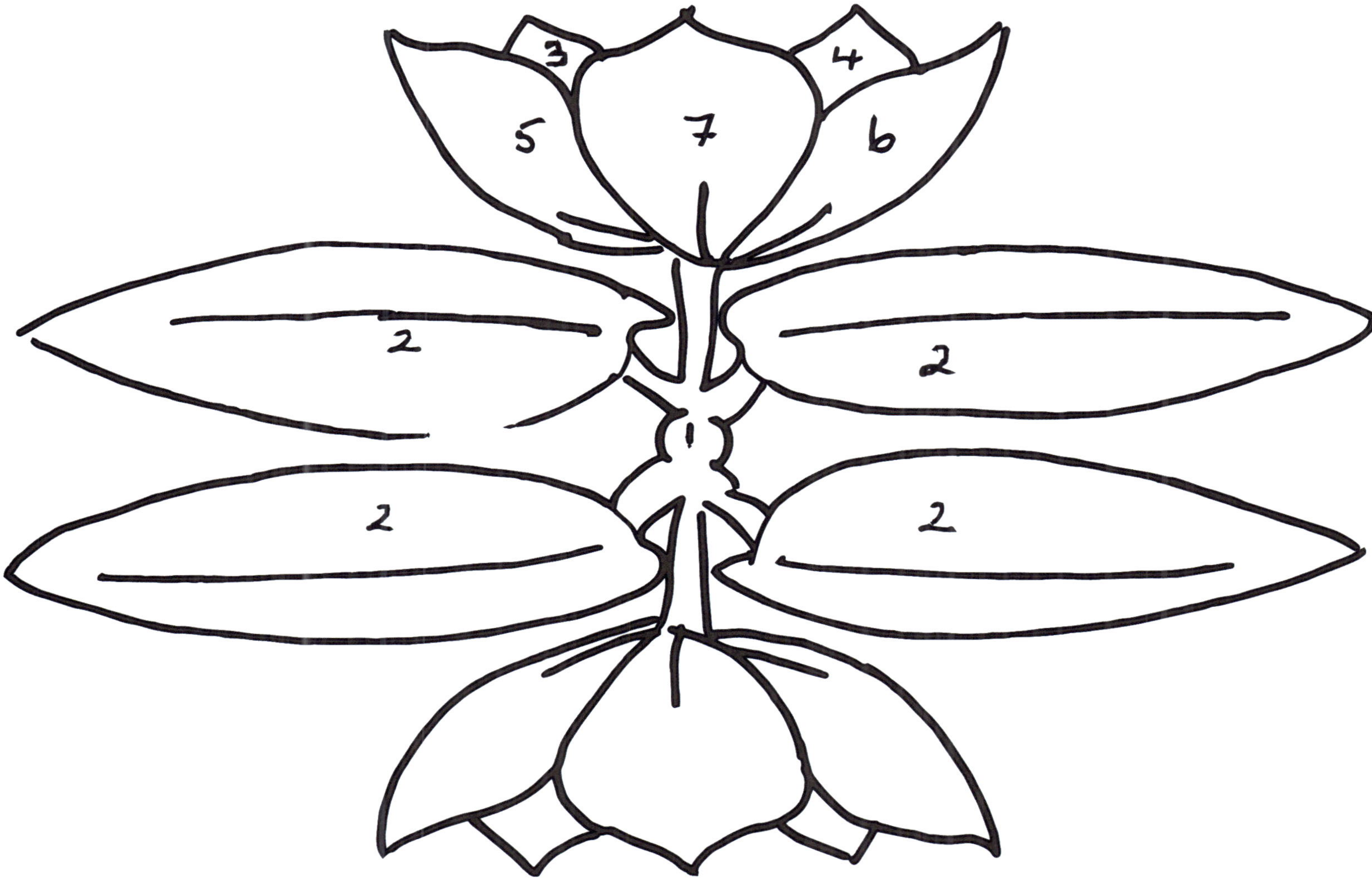

Hand Appliqué Hints & Tips

- The petals can be cut as one complete flower (pieces 3, 4, 5, 6, and 7) and then use machine embellishment to define the individual petals. This method does not allow for a variation in the color shading on some of the insides of the petals (pieces 3 and 4).
- The stem (piece 1) and the four leaves (piece 2) can be cut as one piece and machine embellished.
- The Water Lily is in water and the lower flower is a reflection — the water can be shown by a row of beads or machine stitching.

Water Lily Border

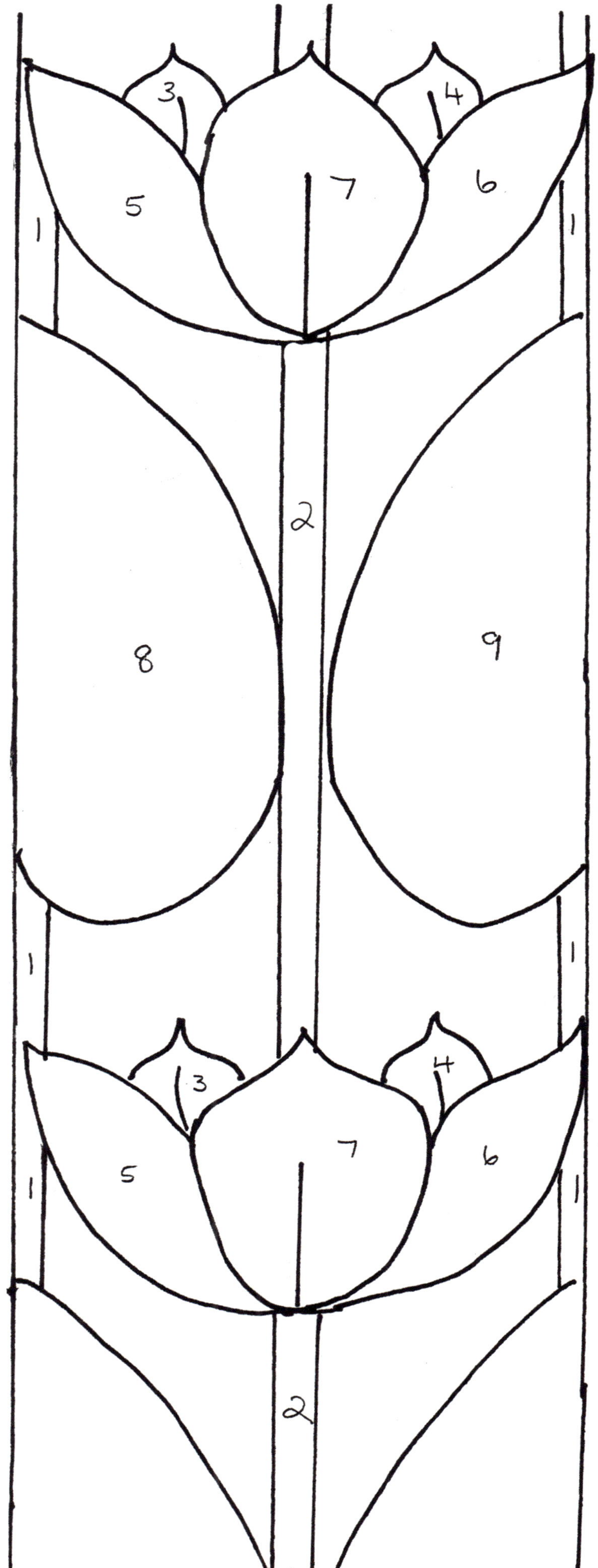

Machine Appliqué Hints & Tips

- Cut the small petals (pieces 3 and 4) 1/8 inch longer to go under pieces 5, 6, and 7.
- Cut pieces marked "1" a scant 1/8 inch longer to go under the leaves and flowers or you can cut and sew one long strip and place the other pieces over the top. The same method can also be used for the pieces marked "2."
- Pieces 5, 6, and 7 can be cut as one complete petal and machine embellished to define the separate petals.
- For the narrow stems use Heat 'n' Bond or similar.
- Stitch and Tear can be used on the reverse of the bloc as a stabilizer.

Woody Nightshade
(Bitter Sweet)

"...The dark full stream by summer long forgot,
The tangled hedges where, relaxed and dead,
The twining plants their withered berries shed,
And feels therewith treachery of the sun,
And knows the pleasant time is well nigh done."

~ *William Morris*

The generic name was first used by Pliny the Elder (or Gaius Plinius Secundus), born 23AD in Italy, for a plant also known as *strychnos*.

In the Middle Ages, the Woody Nightshade, second name, *Dulcamara*, was written as Ammaradulcis, signifying literally "bittersweet," the common county name given to the fact that the root and stem, if stewed, tasted first bitter and then sweet and to its use as a symbol of fidelity and to repel evil. Collars of Woody Nightshade were worn by people and their animals to avert witchcraft, and a necklace containing its berries was found in the tomb of Tutankhamen.

In Lincolnshire, garlands of bittersweet were once hung on pigs to protect them from witchcraft.

An alkaloid in the plant is said to give its berries a bitter taste before turning sweet, giving the plant its alternative name, Bitter Sweet. It causes sickness if eaten.

The Woody Nightshade flowers are a brownish/dark violet on the outside and yellow/green on the inside with violet veins, yellow stamens, and dull green leaves. The fruits, an ovoid, cone-shaped berry, are green, which turn to yellow and then red with yellow antlers.

Woody Nightshade Single Flower

Machine Appliqué Hints & Tips

- Cut leaves (pieces marked 6) as a whole piece.
- Add a 1/8 inch to the top end of the stem when cutting out piece marked "5," as this piece goes under the "cup" (pieces marked 2, 3, and 4).
- The piece marked "4" can be added to the stem when you cut the pieces (piece marked 5). Use machine embellishment to define the fruit cup.

Woody Nightshade Multi Flower

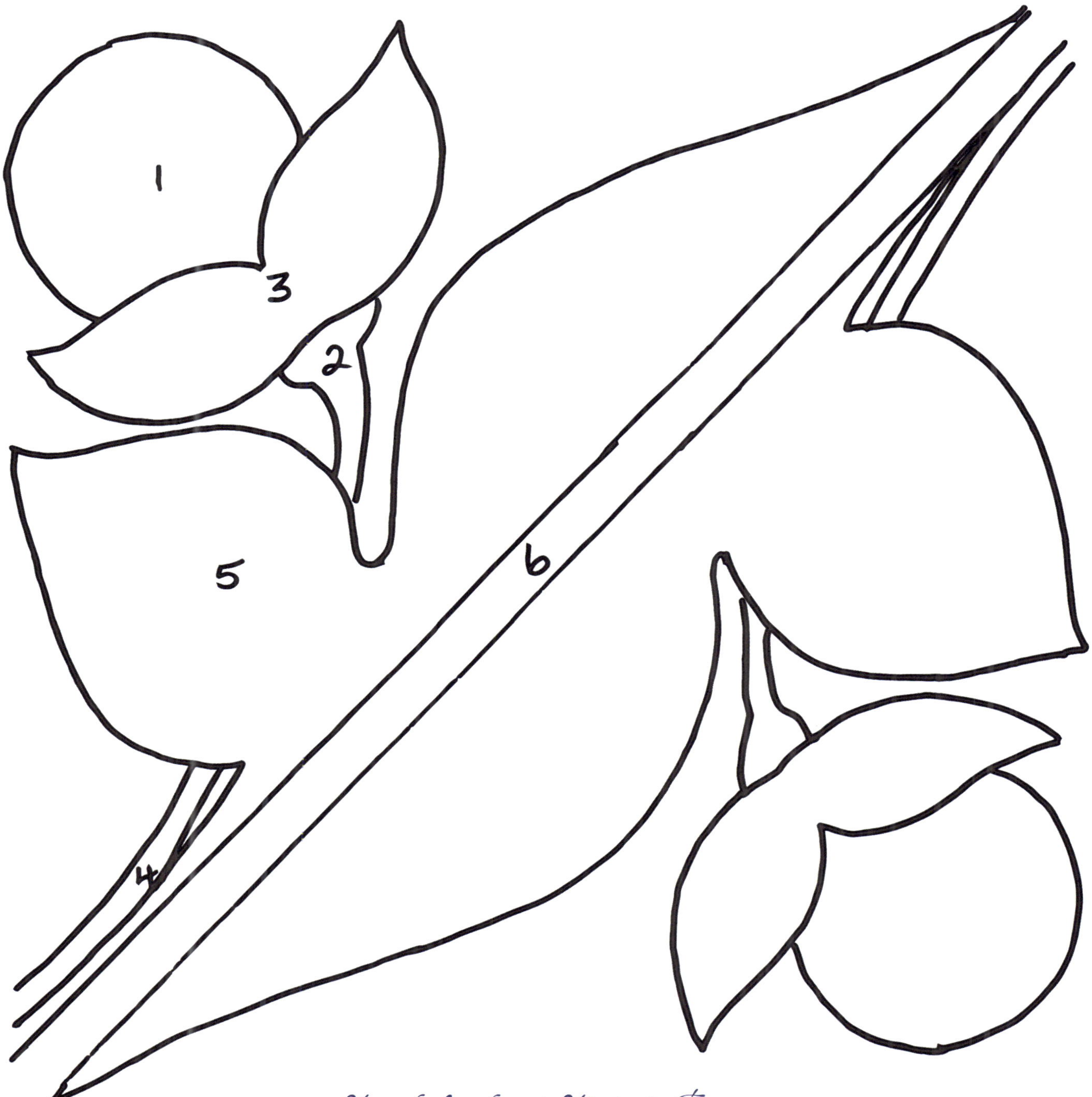

Hand Appliqué Hints & Tips

- With this block, it is essential to get the center point correct.
- Freezer paper appliqué may help with this block.
- To balance this block, two additional seed heads and "cups" have been added to the end of stems (see color picture of block).
- Add a scant 1/8 inch to the ends of the stem (piece 2) — this piece goes under the pieces marked "3" and "5," but the stem (piece 4) can be extended to join piece 2 and placed underneath the leaf marked "5" before sewing.
- The bottom part of the block is a mirror image of the top and completed in the same order.
- If you wish to add the other two fruits and cups to the ends of the piece marked "6," piece 6 must be sewn first.

Woody Nightshade Border

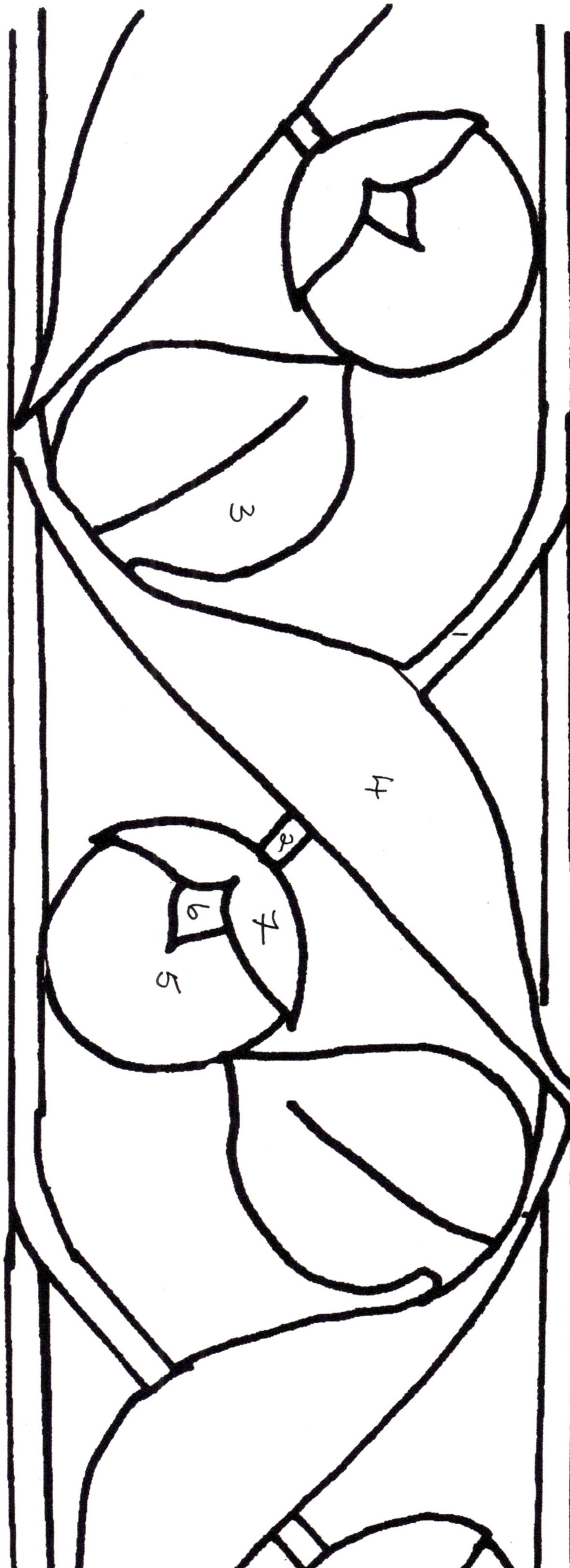

Machine Appliqué Hints & Tips

- Using freezer paper helps with the construction of this block.
- Add a scant 1/8 inch extra to both ends of the piece marked "1" as it goes under the flower and piece "7."
- The tulip petals (pieces 2, 3, and 4) can be cut as one complete flower. When applied, they can be machine embellished to define them.
- If constructing the flower separately, begin by stitching the stem (piece 1) and the middle petal (piece 2) and then the two remaining petals, overlapping one petal at the center join (pieces 3 and 4).
- Stitch the two leaves in place (pieces 5 and 6).
- The bottom border strip (piece 7) can be finished 1/2" wide.

Border Block Wall-Hanging

Embellishments

You can embellish the flowers and leaves using many techniques, including beads, sequins, buttons, ribbons, lace, and hand and machine threads.

Using different threads creates different effects; hand-sewing threads include embroidery cottons (6 stranded), metallic embroidery threads (6 stranded), and Cotton Perle (single stranded), which ranges in thickness from No.3 to No. 12 (12 the finest) — all the above are now available in variegated colors. For machine sewing, there are cotton threads (matte finish), polyester or polyester spun with cotton threads (shinier than the cotton thread), metallic threads (shiny finish), and new holographic and variegated threads. Beads are available in all shapes, sizes, and colors: plain glass, fancy glass, crystal, plastic, ceramic, and wood. Buttons stitched on with beads also give a simple and effective embellishment.

The close-up pictures on these pages show some of the embellishments used in the blocks. You can copy the embellishments or undertake your own embellishments to personalize your own Mary's Garden Quilt.

Planting a Mary's Garden

As the mother of Christ, Mary was honored by having a number of plants named after her, which could be planted in Mary's Garden. On the next two pages are a few plants that you can add to the flowers included in this book to help you get started on your own "Mary's Garden."

1. Rose

The rose symbolizes Mary as the Queen of Heaven. The red rose represents sorrow. The white rose shows joy, and the yellow rose stands for the honor bestowed upon Mary.

2. Violet

The violet is a symbol of modesty and simplicity; humble acceptance to the words from the angel Gabriel: "Let it be done unto me according to your will."

3. Carnation

Legend says that the carnation bloomed on the night of Jesus' birth — a sign of Mary's joy at the Child's birth.

4. Oxeye Daisy

It is said that when the Wise Men reached Bethlehem, they looked for another sign to guide them to the new king. King Melchior saw a white and gold flower and knew which building to enter.

5. Forget-me-not

The tiny blue flowers of this plant represent Mary's eyes.

6. Lavender – Breath of Paradise

This fragrant plant represents purity, cleanliness, and virtue — Mary's spotlessness and chastity. It had no scent until Mary, it was said, laid Jesus' swaddling clothes on the bush.

7. Marigold

Early Christians placed marigolds around statues of Mary in place of coins, calling them Mary's gold.

8. Bluebells

These bell-shaped flowers resemble tiny thimbles and represent Our Lady's working hands. They were often called Our Lady's Thimbles.

9. Speedwell

This plant is also known as Mary's Resting Place. Legend has it that its blossoms marked each spot where the Blessed Mother rested during the flight into Egypt.

10. Lily of the Valley

Lily of the Valley is called Our Lady's Tears. It is said that her tears fell at the foot of the cross and turned into tiny fragrant blossoms. It is also called "Ladder to Heaven," as suggested by the arrangement of the bell-like flowers that always nod on one side of the stalk.

11. Iris

The Iris is a flower, like the Lily, that represents the Annunciation.

12. Fuchsia

These gently drooping flowers resemble pendant earrings. It is said that the child Jesus playfully hung these flower "jewels" on his mother's ears.

L. PUGH.

Sources

Heilmeyer, Marina. *The Language of Flowers: Symbols and Myths*. London, England and New York, New York: Prestel Publishing, 2001.

Hollis, Jill & Cameron. *Poems of the Seasons*. New York, New York: Viking Publishers, 1992.

Mabey, Richard. *Flora Britannica: The Concise Edition*. United Kingdom: Chatto & Windus, 1998.

Pavord, Anna. *The Naming of Names: The Search for Order in the World of Pltants*. London, England: Bloomsbury Publishing, 2005.

Pickles, Sheila. *The Language of Flowers*. New York, New York: Harmony Books, 1990.

The Language of Flowers. M. Joseph, publisher, 1913.

Acknowledgments

I was joint co-ordinator of "A Gift of Quilts," a London 2012 Olympic & Paralympic Games project that took over four years of my life. My long-suffering husband, Doug, was disappointed not to see his name in the book of the project, so I intend to rectify it in this book — none of the projects and books would have been possible without his help, support, and patience, and I would like to say "Thank you, Doug."

This book also could not have been possible without the help of the following quilters who rallied around to help make the blocks:

Anne Brock * Anne Buckler * Barbara Campbell * Christine Dobson * Diane Haynes * Helen Elgar * Jane Hyde * June Whitney * Kath Bedford * Mary Short * Maureen Hearn * Pat Simmonds * Rosemary Furnell * Sharon Garrick * Sue Bone * Tiddly Dyke Quilters

Special thanks goes to Mandy Parks (The Quilt's Whiskers), who has managed to quilt all the tops despite having a full diary of quilts booked in — and still managed to make time for her own personal quilt making.

To Lynne Pugh, a good neighbor and artist... She has undertaken all the paintings used in this book. Lynne has been artist-in-residence for the "Spring Gathering" (a large Christian gathering that takes place over Easter each year) and runs short courses, day classes, one-to-one tutoring, and also undertakes commissions.